TRAVERSE THEATRE

Traverse Theatre Company
presents

Milk

by Ross Dunsmore

First performed at the Traverse Theatre, Edinburgh,
on 7 August 2016

A Traverse Theatre Company Commission

Milk

Cast

CYRIL	**Cliff Burnett**
DANNY	**Ryan Fletcher**
NICOLE	**Melody Grove**
STEPH	**Helen Mallon**
ASH	**Cristian Ortega**
MAY	**Ann Louise Ross**

Creative Team

Writer	**Ross Dunsmore**
Director	**Orla O'Loughlin**
Designer	**Fred Meller**
Lighting Designer	**Philip Gladwell**
Composer/Sound Designer	**Danny Krass**
Choreography	**White & Givan**
Voice Coach	**Ros Steen**
Assistant Director	**Amy Gilmartin**

Production Team

Production Manager	**Kevin McCallum**
Chief Electrician	**Renny Robertson**
Deputy Electrician	**Claire Elliot**
Head of Stage	**Gary Staerck**
Lighting & Sound Technician	**Tom Saunders**
Company Stage Manager	**Gemma Turner**
Deputy Stage Manager	**Naomi Stalker**
Assistant Stage Manager	**Rosie Ward**
Costume Supervisor	**Sophie Ferguson**

Foreword

from Director Orla O'Loughlin

Every now and then a play arrives out of the blue and changes everything. *Milk*, the first full-length play by Ross Dunsmore, is one of those plays.

I remember sitting down at my desk about eighteen months ago and coming face-to-face with a very deliberately placed printed copy of *Milk*. Andy McNamee, our trainee director at the time, put his head round my door, nodded at the script and said, 'I think you'll like this!' He was right. I knew as soon as I read it that the Traverse had to produce it.

I have worked with Ross since then to bring his vision to our stage. As the work has evolved the entire team at the Traverse has become profoundly invested in his play. There has been a pervasive feeling that we are engaged in something important. Not simply because it is an extraordinary play, but because it represents the perfect fulfilment of what we exist to do: to find, nurture and give a powerful platform to those writers who have something vital to say about where we as a society find ourselves today.

Milk came to the Traverse during our Open Submissions window, when we invite playwrights to send us their work. We read every play submitted to us. We are one of very few theatres in the UK to make this commitment. At this moment it feels more crucial than ever to keep our doors open to as many voices as we can. We live in an era where Open Submissions could be classed as an 'additional' activity for an austerity-bitten sector. To resource Open Submissions at this time is effectively, as one of our Associate Artists, Tim Price, put it, 'an act of resistance . . . a refusal to pull the ladder up on those writers who may be isolated by an number of complicated factors that can remove people from culture.' You don't need to be on attachment. You don't need a friend or relative in the industry. You don't need to be known. You just need to write and the Traverse will treat you as a writer. Open Submissions is the least fashionable, least visible activity a theatre can offer. Yet it is the only way we can guarantee all voices are heard. It costs a fortune but *Milk* proves we can't afford not to do it.

Although *Milk* tells the story of six individuals, and their relationships, it's ultimately an exploration of community. Most importantly it examines the power of our shared experience and asserts that hope can flourish even in the most desperate circumstance.

Huge thanks to Ross for sending us *Milk* and trusting us with it. Thanks too to one of the most inspiring acting and creative ensembles it has been my privilege to lead.

I hope that you experience even a fraction of the revelation and joy we have had in bringing this timely and beautiful play to you.

Company Biographies

Cliff Burnett (Cyril)

Previous work for the Traverse Theatre includes: *Fall, Three Musketeers and the Princess of Spain* (English Touring Theatre/Traverse Theatre/Belgrade Theatre, Coventry) and *Accounts* (Traverse Theatre/Riverside Studios). Other theatre includes *This Restless House* (Citizens Theatre/National Theatre of Scotland); *Lot and His God, Into That Darkness, A Christmas Carol, Hamlet* (Citizens Theatre); *As You Like It, Romeo and Juliet, A Midsummer Night's Dream, Hamlet* (RSC); *Caledonia, Let The Right One In* (National Theatre of Scotland);*The Government Inspector* (Communicado/Tron); *An Argument About Sex* (Untitled Projects/ Tramway); *Peer Gynt* (Dundee Rep/National Theatre of Scotland/Barbican); *Romeo and Juliet, The Cherry Orchard, Equus, Moby Dick Rehearsed, The Tempest, Hedda Gabbler* (Dundee Rep); *Othello* (Byre Theatre); *Genius, The Merchant of Venice, Cabaret, A View from the Bridge, Dracula, Bring Me Sunshine* (Newcastle Playhouse); *Hamlet* (Leicester Phoenix); *Guise* (Royal Court); *Look Back in Anger* (Queen's Theatre, Hornchurch); *Hapgood, Pygmalion, Taking Steps, The Picture of Dorian Gray, Gaslight, Abigail's Party, Absurd Person Singular* (Century Theatre).

Film and television credits include: *The Paradise, Bergerac, Let Justice be Done* (BBC); *Emmerdale, Wilderness Edge, Menace Unseen, Inside Story, Shine on Harvey Moon, Last Place on Earth, Brilliant Love* and *A Prayer for the Dying*.

Radio credits include: *Fall, Break My Bones, Listen to the Singing, Accounts, Epsom Downs, The Machine Stops* and *Hassan*.

Ross Dunsmore (Writer)

Ross is from Glasgow. He trained as an actor at RADA and has since worked extensively in theatre, film and television, including productions with the National Theatre of Scotland, Theatre Clwyd, Chichester Festival Theatre, Sheffield Crucible, the Bush Theatre, Borderline Theatre Company, TAG, the Tron, the Finborough and the Young Vic.

As a writer he took an MA in Film at the University of London before spending a year studying playwriting with John Burgess, former Head of New Writing at the National Theatre. One of the winners of the Scotland Short Play Award 2015, his short works for theatre have also been performed in London, Milan and New York. *Milk* is his first full-length play.

Ryan Fletcher (Danny)

Previous work for the Traverse includes: *The Last Witch*. Other theatre credits include *The Choir* (Citizens Theatre); *The Driver's Seat, Blackwatch, The Wheel, Cockroach, 365, Wolves In the Walls, Roman Bridge, Nobody Will Ever Forgive Us* (National Theatre of Scotland); *Othello* (Frantic Assembly); *Once* (Original Cast, Phoenix Theatre); *The Infamous Brothers Davenport* (Vox Motus/Royal

Lyceum); *Prom, Midsummer Night's Dream, Cyrano de Bergerac, Turbo Folk, Before I Go, Waterproof* (A Play a Pie and a Pint); *Beautiful Burnout* (National Theatre of Scotland/Frantic Assembly); *The Corstorphine Road Nativity* (Edinburgh Festival Theatre Company); *Confessions of a Justified Sinner* (Royal Lyceum).

Ryan's television credits include: *Gary Tank Commander, Limmy's Show, Scottish Killers, Filthy Rich, Taggart, River City* and *Stop, Look, Listen*.

Philip Gladwell (Lighting Designer)

Philip's previous work for the Traverse includes: *Swallow, Ciara, I'm With the Band, The Arthur Conan Doyle Appreciation Society, In the Bag* and *Melody*. Other credits include: *Cymbeline* (Royal Shakespeare Company); *The James Plays* (National Theatre of Scotland); *The World of Extreme Happiness, Love the Sinner* (National Theatre); *After Miss Julie* (UK tour); *Mr. Burns, Before the Party* (Almeida); *Fraulein Julie* (Schaubuhne/Barbican); *Blanc de Blanc* (Sydney Opera House); *Laila* (UK tour); *The Seagull* (Regent's Park); *The Twits, Liberian Girl, God Bless the Child, The Ritual Slaughter of Gorge Mastromas, No Quarter, Kebab* (Royal Court); *A Midsummer Night's Dream* (Barbican); *Hairspray* (UK tour); *Jackie the Musical* (UK tour); *First Love is the Revolution, The Boy Who Fell into a Book, Pastoral* (Soho Theatre); *The Sound of Music, Gypsy, The King and I, Chicago* (Curve Leicester); *Limbo* (London/international tour); *The Member of the Wedding* (Young Vic); *Testing the Echo* (Out Of Joint); *Gobsmacked* (Edinburgh Festival Fringe/international tour); *The Rise and Fall of Little Voice* (Birmingham Rep/West Yorkshire Playhouse); *Enjoy* (West Yorkshire Playhouse); *The Infidel* (Theatre Royal Stratford East); *Mogadishu, Punk Rock* (Lyric Hammersmith); *One For the Road, Hedda Gabler, The Duchess of Malfi* (Theatre Royal Northampton); *The Fahrenheit Twins, Low Pay? Don't Pay!* (Told by an Idiot); *If Only* (Chichester); *1984, Macbeth, Too Clever by Half, You Can't Take it With You* (Royal Exchange); *Terminus* (Abbey Theatre).

Melody Grove (Nicole)

Melody trained at the Royal Conservatoire of Scotland. Her theatre credits include: *The Iliad, Of Mice and Men, The Importance of Being Earnest* (Royal Lyceum); *The Air That Carries the Weight* (Stellar Quines); *Farinelli and The King,* for which she was nominated for a Best Supporting Actress Olivier Award 2016 (Duke of York's/Sam Wanamaker Playhouse); *Light Boxes* (Grid Iron); *Much Ado About Nothing* (Old Vic); *The Strange Undoing of Prudencia Hart* (Royal Court/National Theatre Scotland); *The Importance of Being Earnest* (Lyric Belfast); *2401 Objects* (Analogue); *Snow White and the Seven De'Wharffs* (Macrobert).

Film credits include: *A Stately Suicide, Venus and the Sun, Cant and Camber* and *Sisters*.

Audiobooks include: *Anne Veronica, Desperate Remedies, A Little in Love,* and *Completely Cassidy*.

Danny Krass (Composer/Sound Designer)

Danny's previous work for the Traverse includes: *Swallow, The Artist Man and the Mother Woman, Quiz Show, Spoiling* and *The Devil Masters.*

Other theatre credits include: *International Waters* (Fire Exit); *My Friend Selma* (Terra Incognita); *Who Cares* (Royal Court); *Magic Sho, The Curious Scrapbook of Josephine Bean, Huff* (Shona Reppe Puppets); *Smokies* (Solar Bear); *The Voice Thief, Stuck, The Ballad of Pondlife McGurk, White, Kes* (Catherine Wheels); *Up to Speed* (Imaginate/Ros Sydney); *The Adventures of Robin Hood* (Visible Fictions/Kennedy Centre); *My House, A Small Story* (Starcatchers); *Peter Pan* (Sherman Cymru); *Skewered Snails, He-La* (Iron Oxide); *Mikey and Addie, Littlest Christmas Tree, Rudolf, Mr Snow, The Little Boy that Santa Claus Forgot* (Macrobert); *The Infamous Brothers Davenport* (Vox Motus/Royal Lyceum); *One Thousand Paper Cranes* (Lu Kemp); *The Day I Swapped My Dad for Two Goldfish, The Tin Forest* (National Theatre of Scotland); *Couldn't Care Less* (Plutôt la Vie/Strange Theatre); *Sanitise* (Melanie Jordan and Caitlin Skinner); *Eat Me* (A Moment's Peace); *Waves* (Alice Cooper).

Helen Mallon (Steph)

Helen trained at the Royal Conservatoire of Scotland.

Previous work for the Traverse Theatre includes: *Class Act, Breakfast Plays 2015* and *Cockroach* (Traverse/National Theatre of Scotland).

Other theatre credits include: *The Admirable Crichton, Whisky Kisses, Passing Places, Miracle on 34th Street* (Pitlochry Festival Theatre); *Be Near Me, Secrets, Tutti Frutti, Roman Bridge, 365, The Wolves in the Walls, The Crucible* (National Theatre of Scotland); *Taking over the Asylum* (Royal Lyceum/Citizens Theatre); *Peter Pan* (Citizens Theatre); *Lettuce and Lovage* (Watermill Theatre); *The Good Soldier* (Theatre Royal Bath); *The Uncertainty Files* (Paines Plough); *Lucky Lady* (Tron Theatre); *Hansel and Gretel* (Arches Theatre).

Television and film credits include: *Rillington Place, Senseless, My Zinc Bed* and *Casualty.*

Fred Meller (Designer)

Fred is a freelance international scenographer and theatre designer. She trained at the Royal Welsh College and received an Arts Council Designers Bursary.

Previous work at the Traverse Theatre includes: the Fringe First award-winning *Swallow.*

Her extensive career includes: work for the Royal Shakespeare Company, Cardboard Citizens, the Almeida, Gate Theatre, Royal National Theatre Studio, Watermill Theatre, Nuffield Theatre, Royal Court Theatre, Young Vic, Kaos and Grid Iron. Fred often works in new writing and in non-theatre spaces such as an old hospital, jam factory, a mortuary, a disused brothel, Victorian labyrinthine

Town Hall cellars, a supermarket distribution complex, and the biggest potting shed in Europe. She has also created a broad and diverse range of work for traditional theatre buildings.

Fred exhibited at the Prague Quadrennial in 1999 and 2003, winning the Golden Triga and was selected to exhibit at the World Stage Design in Toronto 2005, and in the National Society of British Theatre Designers exhibitions. Her work is part of the V&A Museum permanent collection. Other awards include: The Jerwood Design Award and a Year of the Artist Award. She is course leader for the BA Performance Design and Practice at Central Saint Martins, University of the Arts, London. She co-convened the Scenography working group at TaPRA (Theatre and Performance Research Association), is a Fellow of the HEA, and a Fellow of the Arts Foundation.

Orla O'Loughlin (Director)

Orla is Artistic Director of the Traverse Theatre. Prior to taking up post at the Traverse, she was Artistic Director of the award-winning Pentabus Theatre and International Associate at the Royal Court Theatre.

Directing work for the Traverse includes: *Tracks of the Winter Bear*, the Scotsman Fringe First and Scottish Arts Club Theatre award-winning *Swallow*, the Scotsman Fringe First award-winning *Spoiling*, the Scotsman Fringe First, Herald Angel and CATS award-winning *Ciara*, *The Devil Masters*, *Clean*, *A Respectable Widow Takes to Vulgarity*, *Fifty Plays for Edinburgh*, *The Arthur Conan Doyle Appreciation Society*, *The Artist Man and the Mother Woman*, and the Herald Angel award-winning *Dream Plays* (Scenes From a Play I'll Never Write).

Other directing work includes: *For Once* (Hampstead Theatre/national tour); *Kebab* (Dublin International Festival/Royal Court); *How Much is your Iron?* (Young Vic); *The Hound of the Baskervilles* (West Yorkshire Playhouse/national tour/West End); *Tales of the Country*, *Origins* (Pleasance/Theatre Severn); *Relatively Speaking*, *Blithe Spirit*, *Black Comedy* (Watermill Theatre); *Small Talk: Big Picture* (BBC World Service/ICA/Royal Court); *A Dulditch Angel* (national tour) and *The Fire Raisers*, *Sob Stories*, *Refrain* (BAC).

Orla is a former recipient of the James Menzies Kitchin Award and the Carlton Bursary at the Donmar Warehouse. She was listed in *The Observer* as one of the top fifty cultural leaders in the UK.

Cristian Ortega (Ash)

Cristian graduated from the Royal Conservatoire of Scotland in 2013.

Theatre credits include: *Little Red and the Wolf* (Dundee Rep/Noisemaker); *The Lion, The Witch and the Wardrobe* (Royal Lyceum); *Squash* (A Play a Pie and a Pint); *Let The Right One In* (National Theatre of Scotland/Royal Court); *King Lear* (Citizens Theatre); *Fleeto* (Tumult in the Clouds).

Film and television credits include: *One Of Us*.

Ann Louise Ross (May)

Ann Louise has appeared in leading roles in most Scottish theatres. She was part of the original ensemble at Dundee Rep Theatre, where she won awards for their productions of *Furthest Than the Furthest Thing*, *Sunshine on Leith* and *The Winter's Tale*. Other productions for Dundee Rep have included: *Much Ado About Nothing*, *Witness for the Prosecution*, *Great Expectations*, *Blood Wedding*, *And Then There Were None*, *Promises Promises*, *Peer Gynt*, *Ubu the King*, *Steel Magnolias*, *Sweeney Todd*, *Mother Courage*, *Romeo and Juliet* and *If Destroyed True*.

Other theatre credits include: *Doctor Faustus* (Citizens Theatre/West Yorkshire Playhouse); *The Guid Sisters* (National Theatre Scotland/Royal Lyceum); *Mary Queen of Scots Got her Head Chopped Off* and *Age of Arousal* (Royal Lyceum).

Film credits include: *Whisky Galore*, *Stone of Destiny*, *Split Second*, *Trainspotting*, *The Witch's Daughter* and *The Acid House Trilogy: Granton Star Cause*.

Television credits include: *River City*, *Katie Morag*, *Shetland*, *Case Histories*, *Bob Servant Independent*, *Rebus: Let It Bleed*, *The Bill*, *The Key*, *Life Support*, *Looking After Jo Jo* and *Hamish Macbeth*. In the course of her career Ann Louise has made many radio drama broadcasts including the lead role of Catrine in the BBC's 1984 classic serial *The Silver Darlings*.

Ros Steen (Voice Coach)

Ros has worked extensively in theatre, film and television. Work for the Traverse includes: *Swallow*, *Ciara*, *The Artist Man and the Mother Wóman*, *The Goat or Who is Sylvia?*, *The Last Witch*, *Damascus*, *Carthage Must Be Destroyed*, *Strangers Babies*, *Tilt*, *Shimmer*, *Dark Earth*, *Homers*, *Outlying Islands*, *Heritage*, *Knives in Hens*, *Passing Places* and *Solemn Mass for a Full Moon in Summer* (as co-director).

Other recent work includes: *The James Plays* (tour); *Macbeth*, *Let the Right One In*, *Glasgow Girls*, *Black Watch* (National Theatre of Scotland); *Cyrano de Bergerac* (Northern Stage/Royal & Derngate); *Fever Dream Southside*, *True West* (Citizens Theatre); *Hedda Gabler*, *Bondagers*, *The Lieutenant of Inishmore* (Royal Lyceum); *Much Ado About Nothing*, *The Cheviot, the Stag and the Black Black Oil*, *Blood Wedding* (Dundee Rep/Graeae/Derby Playhouse), *Great Expectations*, *In My Father's Words* (Dundee Rep); *A Walk at the Edge of the World*, *Sex and God*, *Walden* (Magnetic North); *Nijinsky's Last Jump* (Chordelia Dance Company).

Television and film credits include: *God Help the Girl*, *I Love Luci*, *Hamish Macbeth*, *Monarch of the Glen* and *2,000 Acres of Sky*.

Radio credits include: *East of Eden*, *Cloud Howe*, *The Other One* (BBC Radio 4).

Ros is an Emeritus Professor at the Royal Conservatoire of Scotland.

White & Givan (Choreography)

Previous choreography work for the Traverse includes: *Tracks of the Winter Bear* and *Swallow*. As performers and choreographers with over twenty-five years of experience, White & Givan Co-Artistic Directors Errol White and Davina Givan have a wealth of experience they have fed into the company since its inception in 2009 under its former name, Errol White Company. They have both performed internationally for many years, working alongside such distinguished directors and choreographers as Rui Horta, Darshan Singh Buller, Richard Alston, Wayne McGregor, Bob Cohan, and Janet Smith among many others. In addition to their extensive performing and repertory work they are respected and valued education practitioners, having spent five years as Artistic and Creative Directors of National Youth Dance Wales, and have taught extensively across the UK. Since 2009 the company has received generous support from Creative Scotland, which has allowed Errol and Davina to share their artistic work and practitioner experience with the Scottish dance community. They've staged three successful and critically acclaimed Scottish tours of *Three Works*, *IAM* and most recently *Breathe*. They are currently engaged in a unique dance company in residence scheme with the University of Edinburgh.

Amy Gilmartin (Assistant Director)

Amy is Leverhulme Arts Scholar and Recipient of the JMK Regional Assistant Director Bursary.

She studied Drama and Theatre Arts at Queen Margaret University, specialising in directing. She is the founder and Co-Artistic Director of Urban Fox Theatre, directing and producing *Globophobia*, *Safeword* and *Heartlands*. Her work as a freelance director includes: *Kiss Cuddle Torture* and *Warrior*, as well as a new adaptation of *Miss Julie* produced by Black Dingo Productions, and many events for Theatre Uncut.

She is currently a member of the Tron 100 and the Traverse Theatre's Directors Programme.

Previous work as Assistant Director includes: *Soup, One Gun* and *Thank God for John Muir* (A Play a Pie and a Pint).

The JMK Trust was founded in 1997 in memory of a theatre director of thrilling promise, James Menzies-Kitchin, who died suddenly and unexpectedly at the age of 28. It runs the annual JMK Young Director's Award and works with theatres around the UK in its regional programme to discover and support emerging theatre directors. The assistant director bursary, funded by the Leverhulme Trust Arts Scholarships Fund, is another part of our work which enables directors to learn new skills through practical experience.

For more details please visit www.jmktrust.org.

Traverse Theatre Company

The Traverse is Scotland's new writing theatre. Formed in 1963 by a group of passionate theatre enthusiasts, the Traverse was founded to extend the spirit of the Edinburgh festivals throughout the year. Today, under Artistic Director Orla O'Loughlin, the Traverse nurtures emerging talent, produces award-winning new plays and offers a curated programme of the best work from the UK and beyond, spanning theatre, dance, performance, music and spoken word.

The Traverse has launched the careers of some of the UK's most celebrated writers – David Greig, David Harrower and Zinnie Harris – and continues to discover and support new voices – Stef Smith, Morna Pearson, Gary McNair and Rob Drummond.

With two custom-built and versatile theatre spaces, the Traverse's home in Edinburgh's city centre is a powerhouse of vibrant new work for, and of, our time. Every August it holds an iconic status as the theatrical heart of the Edinburgh Festival Fringe.

Outside the theatre walls, it runs an extensive engagement programme, offering audiences of all ages and backgrounds the opportunity to explore, create and develop. Further afield, the Traverse frequently tours internationally and engages in exchanges and partnerships – most recently in Quebec, New Zealand and South Korea.

'The Traverse remains the best new writing theatre in Britain.'
(The Guardian)

For more information about the Traverse please visit

www.traverse.co.uk

With thanks

The commission of *Milk*, by Ross Dunsmore, was kindly supported by Alan and Penny Barr.

The Traverse Theatre extends grateful thanks to all those who generously support our work, including those who prefer their support to remain anonymous.

Traverse Theatre Supporters
Diamond – Alan & Penny Barr, Katie Bradford
Platinum – Angus McLeod, Iain Millar, Nicholas & Lesley Pryor, David Rodgers
Gold – Carola Bronte-Stewart, Helen Pitkethly
Silver – Judy & Steve, Bridget M Stevens, Allan Wilson

Trusts and Foundations
Edinburgh Airport Community Board
The Andrew Lloyd Webber Foundation
The Binks Trust
The Cross Trust
The Dr David Summers Charitable Trust
The James Menzies-Kitchin Memorial Trust
The Saltire Society
Unity Theatre Trust

Corporate Supporter
Arthur McKay

Traverse Theatre Production Supporters
Cotterell & Co
Paterson SA Hairdressing
Signarama
Rouge Flowers

Special thanks go to
Greta Canny, Andy McNamee, Jo Rush, Tam Dean Burn, Keith Fleming,
Anne Lacey, Gail Watson, Mr Taylor and Ms Whitfield at Knox Academy,
Toby Beaven, Co-op Food, The Lyceum Theatre, Theatre Stuff, The Clyde Service
and all those who have helped and supported *Milk*.

Grant funders

FUNDED BY
·ƐDINBVRGH·
YOUR COUNCIL – YOUR CITY

ALBA | CHRUTHACHAIL

Traverse Theatre – the Company

Milk

Ross Dunsmore is from Glasgow. He trained as an actor at RADA and has since worked extensively in theatre, film and television including productions with the National Theatre of Scotland, Theatre Clwyd, Chichester Festival Theatre, Sheffield Crucible, the Bush Theatre, Borderline Theatre Company, TAG, the Tron, the Finborough and the Young Vic. As a writer he took an MA in Film at the University of London before spending a year studying playwriting with John Burgess, former Head of New Writing at the National Theatre. His short works for theatre, including one of the winners of the Scotland Short Play Award 2015, have also been performed in London, Milan and New York. *Milk* is his first full length play.

ROSS DUNSMORE

Milk

ff

FABER & FABER

First published in 2016
by Faber and Faber Limited
74–77 Great Russell Street,
London WC1B 3DA

Typeset by Country Setting, Kingsdown, Kent CT14 8ES
Printed and bound by CPI Group (UK) Ltd, Croydon CR0 4YY

A CIP record for this book
is available from the British Library

ISBN 978-0-571-33422-3

2 4 6 8 10 9 7 5 3 1

For Deborah

My dad was a kind man. When I was eleven he gave me a poem. Above it he'd written, 'The greatest thing you'll ever learn is just to love and be loved in return.' At the time I hadn't the faintest idea what he meant. Now, at least in part, I think I do. We all need to be nourished, to be held, to be loved, but perhaps within us there is an even greater need to love and nourish others in return, and when this need is compromised or devalued by fear or mistrust, as individuals and as a society we are diminished.

I would like to thank Orla O'Loughlin,
John Burgess and Jo Rush for their support
and encouragement in the writing of this play

Milk was first performed at the Traverse Theatre, Edinburgh, on 7 August 2016. The cast, in alphabetical order, was as follows:

Cyril Cliff Burnett
Danny Ryan Fletcher
Nicole Melody Grove
Steph Helen Mallon
Ash Cristian Ortega
May Ann Louise Ross

Director Orla O'Loughlin
Set Designer Fred Meller
Lighting Designer Philip Gladwell
Sound Designer Danny Krass
Movement White and Givan
Voice Coach Ros Steen
Assistant Director Amy Gilmartin

Characters

Steph
fourteen-year-old girl

Ash
fourteen-year-old boy

Danny
thirty-five

Nicole
thirty-seven

Cyril
ninety-three

May
ninety-three

MILK

SCENE ONE

The street.
  Steph and Ash, both fourteen, both in school uniform.

Steph I'm gonna design clothes.

Ash Awesome. You got a good eye.

Steph But I'll be like a singer as well, and a model. And do acting, in movies, but just like big movies, like *Star Wars* or something. And I'll do charity stuff, like a presenter, but dead famous. And I'll go and help in Africa, help all the babies and shit. And I'll be dead serious and clever and I'll cry and I won't wear any make-up. But I'll still look amazing.

Ash I'm gonna make games.

Steph Yeah. You should totally make games. You're clever.

Ash Have a weird name that's just like a line or a shape, and live in Japan or America or under the sea, and just be totally ripped.

Steph I'm gonna marry a DJ, proper grown-up, like thirty or something but still hot. And we'll adopt. Little black baby, little African. Like go to Africa and bring him back in a Gucci bag.

Ash And I'll have this private jet, total Xbox on this private jet, playing Fruit Ninja on a plasma ball, and doing rap and shit, and making movies.

Steph We should do a movie together.

Ash We should totally do a movie together.

Steph I'll do the clothes.

Ash And I'll do the music.

Steph And I'll sing it.

Ash And I'll turn it into a game. And a religion.

Steph Then I'll have a drug problem, but I'll get past it, and I'll be an alcoholic, but I'll get past it and I'll be depressed, but I'll get past it, and I'll adopt like loads more African babies.

Ash And I'll retire at like twenty. And grow wings and have a DS planted inside my head.

Steph And I'll drown.

Ash And I'll explode.

Steph And I'll kill you.

Ash And I'll kill you back.

Steph And I'll eat all my African babies. (*Pause.*) But I'll still look amazing.

SCENE TWO

The IKEA flat.
Danny, thirty-five, is just back from work. Nicole is thirty-seven and heavily pregnant.

Nicole Good day?

Danny Nobody died. First year threw a fire extinguisher at the Assistant Head.

Nicole Nice.

Danny You?

Nicole Lay on the floor. Sat on my ball. Walked round the park. Nothing. Not a twinge. I'm going to be pregnant for ever, baby's going to be bigger than me.

Danny Offer stands. Sex. Get things moving.

Nicole You are truly hilarious. What d'you have for lunch?

Danny Hummus.

Nicole And?

Danny Mars bar.

Nicole Lovely.

Danny Been looking at names?

Nicole God no. I wrote a poem. To my breasts.

Danny Really? Can I see? The poem.

She starts flicking through her iPad.

Nicole They're huge. All veins and chocolate nipples. I even took a picture. And they're getting such an attitude. They've started to look people in the eye, quite rude actually. D'you know, if they could talk, I think they'd sound like a military man with a megaphone. They're just so *there*. You should feel them.

Danny Yes, I should.

Nicole They're being reassigned.

Danny To poetry.

Nicole To baby. (*Finds the poem.*) Do you want to hear my poem?

Danny I'd love to hear your poem.

She reads off the iPad.

Nicole 'Mangrabbers, late to come, but strong. Vest pushers, heavy in your orb gaze, now changing, star gazing, soon to fill and feed. Life-giving, love-guzzling, fountains for baby mouth. Splish, splash, splish, splash.'

Danny (*pause*) That's a beautiful poem.

Nicole I should send it somewhere. *Woman's Hour*. Be a breast poet.

Danny Absolutely.

She cups one of her breasts in one hand. Danny can't help but stare.

Nicole I've never really liked my breasts, but now I think I'm sort of falling in love with them. Now they're going to be useful.

Danny They've always been useful. Can we actually stop talking about your breasts now?

Nicole Were you breast-fed?

Danny I doubt it.

Nicole Nor me, that's why I'm allergic to cats. (*Pause.*) I actually had an epiphany today, just after Melvyn Bragg. I was looking at the clouds through that tree and I suddenly thought, that's really all there is. Feeding and being fed. Everything comes down to that, don't you think? Breast milk, it's like God. (*Pause.*) Those ancient little figures, the little goddesses with the big hips and the droopy tits, that was sort of where it all started, worshipping something, the fact that one human being can nourish another, I mean really there's nothing else, is there? You know, love is milk, that's what it is, love is milk. (*Pause.*) And I'm going to be a goddess.

The prefab.
  A single candle. Cyril and May, both ninety-three, in separate chairs. May is covered in blankets to keep her warm. Cyril wears a coat and holds an empty shopping bag. He's out of breath.
  After a moment:

Cyril Bin.

May Bin?

Cyril Black bin.

May (*pause*) Is there a black bin?

Cyril Past the bus stop.

May Past the bus stop? (*Pause.*) Well, that's good. No, that's good.

Cyril . . .

May So did you see it?

Cyril Bread's on a rack. By the front now. White. Brown. Rolls. (*Pause.*) Baguettes.

May Baguettes?

Cyril Baguettes.

May Oh, I like a baguette.

Cyril Well I like a baguette, you know that. (*Pause.*) First thing 11th Armoured did out of Normandy.

May I know.

Cyril First thing. Rolled into Colleville and they all came out. 'Star Spangled Banner', thought we were Yanks, well

19

you know. And this one comes up and says, 'Pour vous, John Wayne,' and she gives me a baguette, and I says 'bread' and she says 'baguette' and I says 'bread' and she says 'baguette'. (*Pause.*) She was pretty though.

May Pretty? Listen to you. What would you do with pretty?

Cyril Sat on the tank like we were having a picnic.

May (*pause*) We had baguettes for my birthday once. Remember? Back in Raglan Street. Remember? And Jean Kirwan's mum said, 'Baguette? What's that, is that a small bag?' And we had that cheese, with the veins. And those dates with the forks. We were ever so continental. (*Pause.*) Lot to be said for the war.

Cyril . . .

May I think I'd like to do that again. Baguettes. For my birthday.

Cyril Well, we will.

May Get them all round.

Cyril We will.

May Round the piano.

Cyril . . .

May (*pause*) So where's the milk? If the bread's at the front now, where's the milk?

Cyril Couldn't see the milk. Just saw the bread. Few tins. Then I came back.

May (*pause*) Well, you got past the bus stop, so I think you did well. (*Pause.*) And you lit that lovely candle for me.

Cyril I had the money. This pocket.

May I know.

Cyril Three pound.

May I know.

Cyril But it's the dogs.

May I know.

Cyril If I got past the dogs –

May Well, you got past the bus stop.

Cyril And the children. The big ones. Fat ones.

May Don't get upset.

Cyril Carry knives. Tucked away. Down the sock.

May Well, they're nothing. Nothing compared to you. Take away those dogs and those knives and they're nothing. They'll never do what you've done. Liberate Europe? Not a chance. (*Pause.*) And you lit that lovely candle for me, that's not nothing.

Cyril (*pause*) They see me coming.

May Oh, I hate them.

Cyril Let the dogs off.

May If I had a gun.

Cyril If I had a tank.

May Hate them. And I'm not like that. Someone should teach them a lesson. Bring them down a peg. Those dogs? Poison them, bleach, that's what my mother did. And the children, poison them all.

The street. Steph and Ash.
  Ash is eating a whole chicken from out of a paper bag.

Steph So you coming round mine or what? My mum's working. Won't get back till like three in the morning. I got vodka.

Ash What's she do then? Your mum.

Steph She's a prostitute. Yeah. Does all the tourists up the West End, two at a time. Comes back with all this Rolex and shit. She even got a yacht up the Bear Marina.

Ash How much she cost?

Steph You can't afford her.

Ash My gran gave me twenty pound for Christmas.

Steph You don't even get to think about my mum for twenty pound.

Ash I'm thinking about her now.

Steph Fuck off.

Ash Up the Bear Marina.

Steph Fuck off!

Ash (*pause*) She's nice your mum. Trim. You should be respectful, not making shit up.

Steph How d'you know I'm making shit up?

Ash She's not a prostitute.

Steph Might as well be. (*Pause.*) I can hear them. Sick. When they're done he goes to the toilet, and on the way back he stops outside my door, every time, just stands there, bare feet. Then in the morning, 'What age you now then?' – that's what he says, 'What age you now?' And he's always looking, put on my uniform and he's always looking.

Ash Maybe he's just looking.

Steph He is not just looking. I know what he wants, I totally know what he wants. Can't believe my mum lets him in the house.

Ash She doesn't let him in for you.

Steph She should give all that shit up.

Ash Why? 'Cause you don't like it?

Steph She's done it, why's she still doing it? She's fucking dried up. And he doesn't want her. I know what he wants. I totally know what he wants, and it's not her.

Ash Still a person.

Steph What's that mean?

Ash Your mum. Just 'cause she's old. Old people still got appetites.

Steph Appetites? Fuck. (*Pause.*) So what's your mum do then?

Ash Sniper. MI6.

Steph Yeah? How come I keep seeing her round Asda?

Ash That's where she hides the bodies, under all them peas.

Steph 'Cause she's got appetites. Fuck me. She has totally got appetites. She is a whale. Buying up all the outta-date food. Little yellow stickers.

Ash . . .

Steph She has a heart attack they're gonna have to drag her to hospital behind a horse.

23

Ash You got a bad mouth.

Steph She is a planet.

Ash Yeah? Better than you. You're not even there. You're like see-through. See your bones.

Steph You wish.

A pause. Ash gets back to eating his chicken.

Are you gonna eat that whole chicken?

Ash Yeah.

Steph That is disgusting.

Ash It's protein. I work out. I need protein.

He continues to eat. Steph watches.

Steph Do you know what they do to chickens?

Ash . . .

Steph They proper fuck chickens up. Make them live in like this sea of shit, in the dark, and they inject them with all these chemicals to make them fat, and when they're so fat they can't even walk, they boil them alive to get the feathers off. And that's true. (*Pause.*) And they make them drink their own piss.

Ash That's why they're so delicious.

She watches him eat for a moment.

Steph (*pause*) So d'you like me, then?

Ash (*awkward*) Yeah.

Steph (*pause*) You can touch me, if you want.

Ash In a bit.

Steph (*pause*) Can I kiss you?

Ash I'm eating chicken.

Steph Well, you coming round mine or what?

SCENE FIVE

The IKEA flat.
   Danny and Nicole try out their new two-way baby monitors. The entire conversation is held through them.

Danny Any large metal object between the baby unit and the parent unit, such as a filing cabinet, metallic doors or reinforced concrete, may block the signal.

Nicole Check.

Danny This product is not a toy.

Nicole Check.

Danny Nor is it a substitute for responsible adult supervision.

Nicole Check.

Danny So is it working?

Nicole Yes, it's working. Everything is working. (*Pause.*) Does baby need a feed?

Danny No, Daddy needs a pint.

Nicole Don't think so.

Danny (*pause*) OK, so this is what it says.

Nicole Enlighten me.

Danny When baby is happy, baby is quiet and baby is green. When baby is sad, baby is loud and baby is red.

Nicole Green happy. Red sad.

Danny That's what it says.

Nicole Check.

SCENE SIX

The prefab.
  May and Cyril, the candle still burning, but smaller now.

May What about a gammon steak? Pineapple on top.

Cyril . . .

May Or a nice chop. What about a nice chop? You used to like a nice chop. (*Pause.*) Home on leave. 'What you got, May? A nice chop'. Lovely.

Cyril . . .

May Even have it on a tray. Nice chop, on a tray?

Cyril . . .

May Or I could do that chicken you like, with the marmalade.

Cyril Chicken? Chicken's a dirty meat.

May (*pause*) Sausages then? Never say no to a sausage.

Cyril Sand. Sweepings off the floor. That's a sausage.

May (*pause*) Fish. Nice bitta fish?

Cyril Bones.

May Take the bones out.

Cyril Never get all the bones out.

May (*pause*) Pie. That's the one. Steak pie.

Cyril Crust.

May Soup.

Cyril Not a meal.

May Space food, like the astronauts have. Meat and two veg in a pill.

Cyril You don't think I get enough pills? I get enough pills.

May (*pause*) I could force-feed you, rubber tube down your throat, tie you to a chair.

Cyril You got a rubber tube? Where you gonna get a rubber tube?

May (*pause*) I could inject you then. Pint of milk straight to your heart.

Cyril Heart's dried up. You'd never find it.

May I could chop off a limb. Boil up your toes.

Cyril Not even hungry.

May Well, you got to eat.

SCENE SEVEN

The park.
  Ash and Nicole. Ash is still eating his whole chicken.
  Nicole watches. After a moment.

Nicole Sorry. Do you have to do that here?

Ash What?

Nicole That.

Ash You think I'm upsetting the ducks?

Nicole (*pause*) And that's a whole chicken. Are you seriously going to eat a whole chicken?

Ash Why, you want some?

Nicole Do you know what they do to chickens?

Ash Why you even looking?

Nicole . . .

Ash (*pause*) I work out. I need protein. (*Pause.*) I'm bulking up.

Nicole Why?

Ash (*pause*) Girls.

Nicole Girls?

Ash Yeah. Girls.

Nicole You think that's what girls like?

Ash No, I know that's what girls like.

Nicole Really.

Ash Yes. Really. (*Pause.*) They say it's all sense of humour and nice eyes, but what they really want is a beast, fucking caveman. So I wanna get big, so I need protein. So do you.

Nicole I don't eat chicken. I know what they do to chickens. And please don't swear.

Ash Dunno what you're missing.

He gets back to eating.

Nicole (*pause*) You're not seriously going to eat that whole chicken are you?

Ash Yes. One a day. Some people do five a day, I do one, one chicken. That's it. That's my food.

Nicole You eat nothing else?

Ash Why you even looking?

Nicole And you think that's good for you?

Ash Could do worse.

Nicole (*pause*) That is not good for you. All that meat. Doesn't your mother tell you? You want to get *big*, you need to eat properly. You need a balanced diet.

Ash I got a balanced diet. I eat both sides of the chicken. Why you bugging me?

Nicole (*pause*) And d'you never think maybe it's a little offensive, eating like that, in public?

Ash It's natural. Man's a carnivore, a predator.

Nicole A predator? Oh, please. Look at you. You didn't catch that chicken. That chicken lived and died in a box.

Ash But if I had to, I would. That's why God gave me claws.

Nicole (*pause*) They inject those with all sorts, you know. You should do some research.

Ash So what d'you eat then?

Nicole A sensible diet. Healthy. Fresh fruit, vegetables. Pulses. It's not rocket science. Just look it up, read a book.

Ash Won't make any difference. City air. Democracy of pollution. I read a book. Your insides are just as fucked up as mine. You got clogged veins and a dirty baby, just 'cause you're standing there.

Nicole I don't have a dirty baby.

Ash Probably got two heads or something.

Nicole Could you please stop!

Ash You started it.

Nicole That's enough!

Ash OK. (*Pause.*) Sorry. (*Pause.*) I'm sure you'll have a beautiful baby.

He wraps up his chicken.

Eat it later then. Don't want you getting stressed.

Nicole (*pause*) Why did you say that? That was a horrible thing to say.

Ash Said I'm sorry.

Nicole And why aren't you at school?

Ash (*pause*) You behaviour management?

Nicole Do I look like behaviour management?

Ash I'm on a study period. I'm in the library. Writing a class presentation on tackling obesity.

Nicole You should be at school.

Ash Well, I will be at school. In a bit. (*Pause.*) So when's the baby coming?

Nicole Soon.

Ash How soon?

Nicole Very soon. (*Pause.*) He was actually due a week ago.

Ash (*pause*) So is something wrong?

Nicole No. Nothing's wrong. Why would something be wrong?

Ash Just logic.

Nicole Baby's late, that's all.

Ash Well shouldn't you be in hospital then?

Nicole I'm not ill. (*Pause.*) And baby's being born at home.

Ash What? In your house?

Nicole Yes. In my house.

Ash (*pause*) But what if it dies?

SCENE EIGHT

The prefab. Cyril and May.
  Cyril now holds a spoon.
  The candle has burned lower.

Cyril Well?

May Went traditional.

Cyril Have you gone to town?

May Of course I've gone to town. That's the way it should be. Man back from work, back from the front, needs a proper meal.

Cyril I bet you've pushed the boat right out.

May Of course I've pushed the boat right out. Might be a war on but we still need to eat. Well sit down. Pull in your chair. Turn off the wireless. Wait . . . (*Closes her eyes.*)

God is great and God is good,
And we thank God for our food.
By God's hand we must be fed,
Give us Lord, our daily bread.

Both Amen.

May Go on then.

Cyril Well, don't mind if I do, May. I don't mind if I do.

He puts the empty spoon into his mouth, holds it there.

May Soup to start. Minestrone. Clear. Salty. And there's a second bowl. And that's not from a tin, that's mine. Onions, carrots, celery. (*Pause.*) Chopped cabbage, wee tin of tomatoes. Spaghetti. (*Pause.*) Then it's salt, pepper, Worcester sauce and a quick game of patience on the kitchen table.

Cyril (*takes out spoon*) That's a good soup.

May I know that's a good soup.

Cyril You could always make a good soup.

May First thing my mother taught me. Way to a man's heart. Warm hands, good soup, and God bless the King.

Cyril Chicken stock?

May Carcase.

Cyril Gone right down to my toes.

May (*pause*) Finished?

Cyril Lovely.

May Well, have a stretch, you're in for a treat.

Cyril You pushed the boat out?

May Of course I've pushed the boat out.

Cyril Blown the bank?

May Of course I've blown the bank. Go on.

Cyril puts his spoon back in his mouth.

Beef, topside, with Yorkshire puddings and gravy right up to the brim. Roast potatoes with crispy bacon, and a fried egg. Some chips in a bowl if you fancy and cauliflower cheese with a crust. And it's all on linen, and it's Sunday. And you've cut the grass, and you've got no pills, and you've got teeth like a bear. (*Pause.*) Tuck in, don't be shy, I like to see a man eat.

Cyril takes out the spoon but holds it by his mouth.

Cyril Now that is good. Make these Yorkshires yourself?

May What kind of question is that?

Cyril Horseradish?

May In the little pot.

Cyril Gravy?

May By your elbow.

Cyril Wouldn't mind another roastie.

May Help yourself, there's more in the oven.

Cyril I'll need a lie-down after this.

May Cheeky.

Cyril holds the spoon in his mouth for a moment, then takes it out.

Cyril (*pause*) Well, that was the best. Best ever.

May Room for pud? It's powdered egg.

Cyril (*pause*) Maybe later.

May It's your favourite.

Cyril Maybe later.

May (*pause*) Don't get upset.

Cyril Shoulda done my bit. That's all. I need to do my bit.

May I know.

Cyril I had the money.

May I know.

Cyril But it's the dogs.

May (*pause*) Well, you lit that candle, and you won the war. Right round the world you went. For me. (*Pause.*) And we had that biscuit, remember? That lovely biscuit. That was you. Don't get upset. You're my hero. Don't get upset.

SCENE NINE

The classroom.
Steph is looking at her phone. Ash sits next to her.

Steph Can't say me.

Ash Dunno.

Steph Can't say dunno. And don't say Chloe Stewart, 'cause that's boring. You have to say something weird, like a teacher or someone's mum or something.

Ash Dunno.

Steph Fuck! What is wrong with you? You're a boy. All you think about is sex.

Ash Why you shouting?

Steph If you don't tell me, I'm gonna shove my fingers in your mouth.

Ash (*pause*) I dunno. Weather girl.

Steph Weather girl?

Ash Yeah. Blonde. Does the weather. She's nice.

Steph Who?

Ash On the telly. Rain. Snow. Dry on Tuesday. How come you're not doing this?

Steph Favourite food? Fuck, don't even bother.

Ash What about you?

Steph I'm not doing it.

Ash Well I'm not doing it then.

Steph (*pause*) OK. Fantasy, Mr Doig. Favourite food, I don't eat.

Ash Mr Doig?

Steph Yeah. Totally.

Ash Like Mr Doig Mr Doig?

Steph Yeah. Why?

Ash He's a freak.

Steph He is not a freak.

Ash He's on the sex offenders' register.

Steph He is not on the sex offenders' register. (*Pause.*) How could he be a teacher if he was on the sex offenders' register?

Ash OK, he *wants* to be on the sex offenders' register. *Mr Doig?*

Steph You jealous or something?

Ash The man looks like a teacher.

Steph He is a teacher. (*Pause.*) And he doesn't look like a teacher. He is fit.

Ash Mr Doig?

Steph Does running, I've seen him. And he's tall.

Ash Since when?

Steph And he's into me.

Ash He's what?

Steph I've seen him looking. I could totally have him.

Ash Wrong.

Steph Not wrong. We got a thing. Feel sorry for him. Sometimes when he looks at me I think he's gonna cry.

Ash That is so sad. That is embarrassing.

Steph (*pause*) Why?

Ash Ask anyone.

Steph What?

Ash Ask.

Steph What?

Ash (*pause*) Chloe Stewart.

Steph Fuck off.

Ash He can't even look her in the eye. Last week she kept putting her hand up and saying, 'Sir, how d'you spell vagina?' I thought he was gonna pass out. He was fucked up. And his wife's pregnant. And I saw him chatting up Miss Roberts and Miss Blakesly after school, *and* he told Stacey Thorpe she had nice eyes, so you're not even top five.

Steph Not true.

Ash True. (*Pause.*) What? Now you jealous?

Steph Fuck off.

Ash You really thought he was into you?

Steph Fuck off.

Ash That is so sad.

Steph Fuck off!

Ash (*pause*) Gimme that phone.

Steph Don't wanna do it.

Ash You started it. Gimme the phone.

He grabs the phone, reads off it.

'What would you change about your body?'

Steph She's done that on purpose –

Ash What would you change?

Steph – and she dresses like a fucking prostitute.

Ash What would you change?

Steph Why you bugging me? Shut up.

Ash What would you change about your body?

Steph (*snaps*) I'd fucking burn it. Cut it up and bury it, then get born again all beautiful and long. And I'd be called Chloe fucking Stewart, and I'd be a fucking weather girl.

Ash (*pause*) You'd be a good weather girl. (*Pause.*) Go on. Do it. Be a weather girl.

Steph Tomorrow will be shit, then the next day will be shit and the weekend will be shit as well. (*Pause.*) With a big drizzle of cocks up the West End.

Ash You're good. You gotta bright future.

Steph (*pause*) So take me out then.

SCENE TEN

The IKEA flat.
Nicole and Danny in bed. Danny rests his hand on Nicole's tummy.

Nicole So you think he's OK?

Danny Yes.

Nicole He's not moving so much.

Danny There's less room.

Nicole So you think he's OK?

Danny Yes.

Nicole (*pause*) And you'll stay with me?

Danny Yes.

Nicole I don't just mean now. I mean always.

Danny Yes.

Nicole Even when I'm really old, and you have to feed me through a straw and take me to the toilet?

Danny Yes.

Nicole And when I don't want to have sex with you any more?

Danny Yes.

Nicole And when I don't know who you are?

Danny Yes.

Nicole And when I'm a really bad mother?

Danny Why would you be a bad mother?

Nicole 'Cause my mother was a bad mother.

Danny Your mother wasn't well.

Nicole (*pause*) I was brushing my teeth this morning, looking in the mirror. Don't know why I look in the mirror when I brush my teeth, it's not as though I'm going to forget where they are. Is it? (*Pause.*) Is it?

Danny You were looking in the mirror.

Nicole I was looking in the mirror. And I was looking at myself like I wasn't me, like I was a different person, and I suddenly thought, she's happy, she's really happy. (*Pause.*) And I am. (*Pause.*) I want you to know that, are you listening? I want you to know that I love you and I love baby and I am going to try so hard to be a good mum, and before I met you I wasn't very happy, but now I am. And I want you to hear that now. Before I go mad.

SCENE ELEVEN

The street.
  Ash and Steph stand together.
  Steph reads off her phone.

Steph 'A young woman searches for intimacy beyond the bounds of traditional sexual limitations, a journey that ultimately proves both fulfilling and empowering. Fearless and uncompromising, *Romance* is a truly sensual essay in cinematic eroticism, highly controversial for its explicit portrayal of male arousal.'

She looks up at Ash.

Metro. Half-seven.

Ash Wait. That's eighteen. That's gotta be eighteen.

Steph So?

Ash You got ID?

Steph They don't even look.

Ash (*pause*) Why d'you wanna see that?

Steph Meant to be beautiful.

Ash I thought we said *Interstellar*.

Steph This is better. It's romantic. (*Pause.*) And they do it, they actually do it. For real.

39

Ash What, like porn? You wanna see a porn film?

Steph It's not a porn film, it's art. Actress in this is a proper actress. She's beautiful.

Ash No way, man. That is wrong. Proper actress is not doing that.

Steph Fuck, you sound like my mum.

Ash She's a proper actress, she doesn't have to be doing that. Why's she doing that?

Steph Maybe she likes it.

Ash What? People looking?

Steph Yeah. You don't know. Girls like all sorts. Worse than boys.

Ash But people looking?

Steph Why not?

Ash (*pause*) Come on. Let's go to *Interstellar*. Then we'll go to Nando's, I gotta voucher.

Steph I don't wanna go to *Interstellar*, I wanna see this. (*Pause.*) I wanna see this with you.

SCENE TWELVE

The prefab.
May and Cyril. May is piled high with more blankets and curtains, only her head now visible.
Cyril is at the window.
The candle is almost burned down to nothing.

Cyril Two. On the corner.

May Maybe they'll go.

Cyril They never go.

May Well, maybe this time they will. (*Pause.*) Big?

Cyril Big.

May How big?

Cyril Bigger than me.

May Dog?

Cyril Can't see.

May Knife?

Cyril Can't see.

May What they doing?

Cyril Just looking.

May Over here?

Cyril Over here.

May (*pause*) Maybe tomorrow then. I don't mind. Really I don't.

Cyril (*nods*) Better tomorrow. I'll be good tomorrow. Promise.

May (*pause*) You done the door?

Cyril . . .

May All the locks?

Cyril All the locks.

May Try again tomorrow then. You'll feel better tomorrow. Come over to me, pull your chair over to me, we'll sit together. I like it when we sit together.

Cyril In a bit.

May (*pause*) Wish they'd bring back the electric though. Be nice for you to sleep in the bed again.

Cyril We don't want the electric.

May If we had the electric we could use the phone. I think we need to use the phone.

Cyril Who you gonna phone?

May Phone that politician. The police.

Cyril Make it worse. They see the police, they know we're here. They'd be up on that roof again. And the petrol. You want fire through the door? Dogs at the window? We just need to be quiet. Keep quiet and we'll be fine. (*Pause.*) And tomorrow. I'll try again tomorrow.

SCENE THIRTEEN

The street.
    Steph and Ash sit on the edge of the pavement, jackets zipped up, hiding their uniforms. They both hold huge bottles of Coke.
    Ash is reading off his phone.
    Steph watches. They both seem a little shell-shocked.

Ash 'Quarter chicken. Half chicken. Whole chicken. Chicken legs. Chicken thighs. Chicken breast. Offer does not include pittas or wraps.'

Steph How come you don't look at me like that?

Ash Like what?

Steph Like those men.

Ash That's a film.

Steph Yeah. So. Still real. Still people. I mean she proper did something to them. That guy in the bed? That was full on. (*Pause.*) Can't act that.

Ash (*pause*) They're French.

Steph So?

Ash I dunno. They look. Stare. French people. It's genetic. All them footballers.

Steph Footballers?

Ash That's what they do. Stare. Big eyes. Like babies or something. Just 'cause I don't stare doesn't mean I'm not thinking about you. I think about you. Inside.

Steph Do you?

Ash Yeah.

Steph Do you?

Ash Yeah.

Steph (*pause*) Do I keep you awake? Do you think about me at night?

Ash Yeah. Sometimes.

Steph (*pause*) What am I doing? When you think about me.

Ash I dunno. Stuff.

Steph What kinda stuff?

Ash Stuff.

Steph (*pause*) And what are you doing? When you think about me.

Ash Can we go to Nando's now?

Steph Not finished this. Chill. (*Pause.*) I'm getting a new nose. Nose like hers. Hate my nose. It's fat. Look like a pig.

Ash That's stupid. Why you saying that? You're really . . . pretty.

Steph *Pretty?* Fuck.

She suddenly stands up. She takes off her jacket and blazer.

Ash What you doing?

Steph D'you think I gotta good body?

Ash There's people looking.

Steph So? (*Pause.*) I know I got shit tits, but the rest.

Ash Yeah. You gotta good body. Put your stuff on. I wanna go.

Steph Which bit you like best?

Ash I dunno. All of you.

Steph Can't say that. You have to say which bit. Legs, bum. Which bit?

Ash I dunno.

Steph You can't say that! Fuck. Which bit?

Ash (*pause*) I like your face. You gotta nice face.

Steph (*pause*) Are you gay?

Ash What?

Steph Boy says face, that means he's gay.

Ash That's Cas, right? Cas is always saying that shit. Is that Cas?

Steph No. (*Pause.*) But he's right. You're always looking at my face. Why you always looking at my face?

Ash You gotta nice face. I like your face. I like you.

Steph But do you?

Ash Yeah.

Steph Proper?

Ash Yeah.

She comes closer to him, stands over him, softening.

Steph You gotta nice face. Nice hair. Can I touch your hair?

She starts to stroke his hair. He's uncomfortable.

What?

Ash People looking.

Steph So? (*Pause.*) You should cut some, give it to me. (*Pause.*) Close your eyes. Close your eyes.

He does so.

What you thinking? Are you thinking about that film? Are you thinking about me?

He is yielding slightly, accepting.

That's alright.

She traces a finger down his cheek –

(*A whisper.*) I like it.

– then tries to push it into his mouth.
He instantly pulls away and stands up.

Ash What the fuck!

Steph What?

Ash What's wrong with you? People looking.

Steph So?

Ash So what's wrong with you?

Steph What's wrong with *you*? Fuck! What is your problem?

Ash Don't have a problem.

Steph You don't even look at me right.

Ash That's stupid.

Steph That's true. Cas, all those boys? I've seen them. That film? That's them. That's the way they look at Chloe Stewart. I mean she proper fucks them up.

Ash Cas?

Steph At least he looks.

Ash Yeah, he looks. He totally looks. Ripped open Stacey's top up the Glades, put it on his phone. That what you want?

Steph Least a boy rips at you, you know he likes you.

Ash You need to see someone, you need a therapist or something.

Steph You don't even touch me. It's like you got no hands.

She grabs him by the hands.

Ash What you doing?

She presses his hands against her body.

Steph Look, you don't do anything. Like a baby.

Ash Get off.

Steph Shitting yourself. Little baby with no hands. Shitting yourself.

Ash What is wrong with you?

Steph You come out. You don't touch me, you don't look at me. I dunno what you want!

Ash I WANNA GO TO NANDO'S!

He suddenly pushes her away, almost a punch.
A beat. She just stares. Then she grabs her stuff.

46

What you doing?

Steph Going.

Ash Where?

Steph When I was seeing Dave Grogan, he used to come round my house, he used to pull at me, even had bruises. My mum had to phone the police.

Ash Is that what you want?

Steph I want something! I wanna man, don't wanna pissy little baby.

Ash A man?

Steph A man.

Ash You are so fucked-up. Look at you! What man's gonna want you?

Steph (*pause, hurt*) Know something? I never even liked you. And you gotta shit face.

Ash Yeah. Whatever.

Steph Yeah. Whatever.

She goes. He calls after her.

Ash I told you we shoulda gone to *Interstellar*! (*Pause.*) Fuck.

SCENE FOURTEEN

The IKEA flat.
  Nicole and Danny. Danny is getting ready to go for a run.

Nicole I was coming back, and there was this mother, walking, dressed up like she was going to a party. And her little boy was behind her and he was shaking, only two, three years old but he was really shaking, and crying so hard. And he was scared. Then the mum turned round and she just screamed at him, 'You fucking little shit, you fucking little shit.' And the little boy started saying 'Sorry, sorry' over and over, but the mum just turned and walked away. Then I saw the little boy had no shoes on, just socks, tiny little socks flat on the pavement. But he started running to keep up, 'cause he wanted his mum, even then, but she just kept on, 'You fucking little shit, you fucking little shit.' Then inside me baby started to kick, really kick, like he was screaming, like he was saying, 'You're a mother, you're going to be a mother, do something.' So I opened my mouth, but there was nothing to come out. She was shouting, and the boy was saying sorry and baby was kicking and screaming inside me . . . but I did nothing. (*Pause.*) Why did I do nothing?

Danny What could you do?

Nicole I will never be that. I will *never* be that. If he cries, if he hurts me, if he hates me, I'll still love him.

Danny I know.

Nicole (*pause*) When I woke up this morning, I forgot I was pregnant, just for half a second. It was awful. (*Pause.*) But then the smells came. That's how you remember. Dust. Something metal. And then I could feel the life right inside me, the blood, right on the surface. And everything flooded back in. All the light and the love. And then I was hungry and I was angry and I was happy and I was drunk. And I was so full of everything, so on the edge of everything, I suddenly wanted sex, can you believe that, I really wanted sex.

Danny So why didn't you wake me up?

Nicole I didn't want sex with you.

SCENE FIFTEEN

The street.

Danny in running gear.

He has just come out of a shop. He holds a plastic bag.

He takes out a bag of crisps, opens them, and stuffs the entire packet in his mouth. He quickly opens a half-bottle of wine and downs it in one go.

He then simultaneously unwraps two bars of chocolate and stuffs them both in his mouth, almost choking.

He slowly becomes aware that Steph is watching him.

Steph Hi, Mr Doig. Could you get me ten B&H, sir? Sorry. They won't sell them to me. They're for my mum. Please, sir. I've had such a shit day.

Danny's mouth is so full he can't speak.

I've got the money. Go on, sir, my mum'll kill me. She's dying for one but she can't get outta bed. She's got ulcers, and a broken leg.

Danny is trying his best to deal with the food in his mouth.

Do you smoke, sir? We could have one each. My mum won't mind. She likes me smoking. And I won't tell no one. Go on, sir. If I don't ask you I'll need to ask some perv who'll probably dump me in his basement or something.

Danny is trying to swallow.

Funny seeing you out of school. You look really different. D'you keep fit, sir? 'Cause you got a nice body. Not being funny. You're not like fat or nothing. D'you go to the gym, sir?

Danny is almost ready to speak.

49

I sit next to Chloe Stewart in your class. She really likes you, says she'd totally run off with you to France or something. But she is a total slag, sir, she's got all diseases, and she's not had a bath since Christmas. And she's done loadsa boys. She let Joe Wood touch her up behind the A block and she even took money for it. Said that made it better. She's fucked-up, she just wants everyone to think she's a total prostitute, which she is, so she doesn't even care. So I wouldn't touch her if I was you, I think you're better than that, and by the way, she totally knows how to spell vagina. (*Pause.*) Can you buy me some? Go on, sir, I'll love you for ever.

Danny's mouth is now empty, but he seems to have nothing to say.

SCENE SIXTEEN

The school.
Ash is giving a presentation to his classmates.
He reads off an A4 sheet of paper.

Ash 'Tackling obesity in children is very important and it is important to educate them about food and getting fat. Children should eat a healthy, balanced diet as this helps them be healthy and do well at school. (*Pause.*) It is also important not to eat too much junk food, but this is a big problem in Britain because everyone does. In 1985 people in Britain spent two billion pounds on junk food. Last year they spent thirty billion pounds, which is a lot more. Body shape has even changed because of this and people now think bigger is better, which is just wrong and not even true, as big people use more electricity and even wear down pavements quicker. Junk food restaurants are the most popular type of restaurant and in my opinion they probably don't even need to advertise any more because they don't have to. (*Pause.*) In my opinion the reason that junk food restaurants are really popular is not because of the food. In my opinion it is because they *really* want you to go there, and that is why everyone does. Even posh people who don't like them still take their kids in after swimming, and business people and kids from private schools and homeless people and old people and gay people and even teachers go there. In my opinion this is because junk food restaurants offer a universal, democratic experience, where everyone sits together and everyone gets to eat the same shit. (*Pause.*) The best food restaurant for good food though is Nando's, who do a lot of different kinds of chicken, and if you say the chicken tastes a bit weird halfway through they'll give you another one. But don't do this in the Nando's on George Street, 'cause that one's mine.'

SCENE SEVENTEEN

The street.

    Danny and Steph outside the shop. They have both just finished a cigarette.

    Steph wears her puffa jacket, unzipped now, over her uniform.

Danny Fuck. I feel sick.

Steph Thought you smoked.

Danny Used to. Stopped for the baby. My wife is having a baby.

Steph I know. (*Pause.*) You'll be a great dad. You got nice eyes, that's how you know.

Danny You think?

Steph I'd love a baby. African baby.

51

Danny What age are you?

Steph Fourteen.

Danny You are a baby.

Steph Same age as Chloe Stewart, you don't think she's a baby.

Danny (*pause, the jacket*) Zip that up. You should get home. And don't tell anyone.

Steph What's she look like. Your wife?

Danny I dunno. My wife.

Steph You still fancy her? Even though she's fat.

Danny She's not fat, she's pregnant.

Steph D'you still love her?

Danny Yes.

Steph D'you love her all the time?

Danny Yes.

Steph D'you still have sex?

Danny (*pause*) I need to get back.

Steph I might adopt. Don't wanna get fat.

Danny It's not fat. It's a baby.

She pulls open her jacket.

Steph D'you think I've got a nice body sir? You can look. It's not weird, just a question.

Danny Zip that up.

She takes her jacket off.

What are you doing?

Steph You can look. It's OK.

Danny Put that on.

Steph (*pause*) Don't you like me, sir?

Danny Put your jacket back on.

Steph Why don't you wanna look? You look at Chloe Stewart.

Danny (*pause*) Go home.

Steph Have I annoyed you, sir?

Danny (*pause*) No. Just . . .

Steph Have I?

Danny No.

Steph I have, haven't I?

Danny No.

Steph (*pause*) Can you kiss me goodbye, sir? Just on the cheek, not being funny, just like a friend, like an uncle or something, go on. (*Pause.*) Please sir. Just to show you still like me.

He hesitates . . . then kisses her on the cheek.
They simply look at each other for a moment.

Are you getting hard, sir?

Danny Go home.

Steph Just asking. It's alright, I like it.

Danny Put your jacket on and go home.

After a moment, she puts on her jacket. As she goes:

Steph I'm gonna dream about you tonight, sir. You're mine now.

The prefab.
  Cyril and May. Cyril is looking out of the window.

May Sweetheart?

Cyril . . .

May Come over, bring your chair over to me. Think I might go for a wee sleep. Think that's it.

Cyril (*pause*) Don't.

May Been in that kitchen all day.

Cyril Not yet.

May But I feel lovely now, not hungry, not cold. And you're here.

Cyril . . .

May I'm very tired.

Cyril You haven't had your baguette.

May Don't think I could eat one now. (*Pause.*) Come away from the window. Come over to me.

Cyril I could try again tomorrow.

May Come away from the window.

Cyril Don't go to sleep.

May But I'm cosy.

Cyril Please. Don't go to sleep.

May (*pause*) I think I have to, sweetheart. Leave the window now. (*Pause.*) Will you kiss me? Tuck me in. And what about that bedtime story? You always said.

Cyril Don't like stories.

May Now you promised me. Go on. (*Pause.*) Not a whole story. Just do the middle, the middle bit, that's the best bit. Go on.

After a moment he leaves the window.

That's the way. Like we said. Come over to me.

With difficulty he drags his chair over next to hers.

That's it. Close.

He sits by her, breathing hard.
She takes off one glove. Slowly, he does the same.
They hold hands.

Well, go on then. Don't have all day.

Cyril (*pause*) Well, they were happy.

May Were they a prince and princess?

Cyril No. They never even met a prince and princess. They met a politician once.

May Well, weren't they lucky.

Cyril (*pause*) They were.

May Go on, sweetheart. Do the story. For me.

Cyril (*pause*) And they lived in Raglan Street. And they had a child. Lived near three years, before it went to Heaven, and for three years they were the happiest people, and every day they ate better than any prince and they loved more than any princess, and they were so full up with such happiness that sometimes bubbles came out of their mouths. And the grass was cut and the washing was drying and wee Douglas was on his blanket. And the sun shone warmer back then. And they knew they were happy because the sadness never stayed, it just rolled on its way, like clouds. (*Pause.*) And that was the middle of things, and for three years they were happy, in the middle of things, and for three years they were full. (*Long pause.*)

You asleep now, May? (*Pause. She is silent.*) You asleep now, sweetheart? (*Pause.*) You give Douglas a big cuddle from me, and I'll be through in a minute.

SCENE NINETEEN

Nicole's baby is born.

SCENE TWENTY

The mum's house.
  Steph holds her phone at arm's length.
  She is filming herself.

Steph There's this bit in *The Hunger Games* where she kisses this boy, but he's got like a fever, so his lips are really hot, and she knows he's sick, he's got like a bug or something, and she knows that's why he's hot. But she doesn't feel it that way, she feels it like he's boiling up for her, like he's been boiling up waiting for her. And that's what I felt when you kissed me, sir, like you've been waiting, like you were hungry. (*Pause.*) Were you hungry, Mr Doig? 'Cause that's how it felt. (*Pause.*) But I know it's impossible, sir, I know you're married and shit and having a baby, and I don't wanna get in the way, so it's like we both just have to let those feelings go, like we know they're there, they'll always be there, but it's just not the right time. (*Pause.*) And that's OK. 'Cause I know you want me now, and that's enough. See you gave me something, sir, gave me that moment. And what you gave me, sir, when you kissed me, you turned me into a woman. My whole life is like changed now, 'cause I felt that hunger, proper, for the first time. And you gave me that. So I want to give you something back, so you'll never forget me.

  She starts slowly to unbutton her top.

The IKEA flat.
  Nicole is no longer pregnant.
  Danny comes in.
  It's quiet.

Danny Hi, Mum.

Nicole Hi, Dad.

Danny You OK?

Nicole I'm counting socks. He has a lot of socks.

Danny (*pause*) D'you want anything?

Nicole No.

Danny Tired?

Nicole No, I'm good.

Danny (*pause*) Been looking at names?

Nicole I wrote a poem. D'you want to hear it?

Danny Maybe later.

Nicole Called 'Ten little fingers, up one little nose'.

Danny Maybe later. (*Pause.*) So you think he's OK? He still won't settle.

Nicole He will. He's gorgeous. How could he be so gorgeous and not settle?

Danny How much did he have?

Nicole It's not an exact science, Danny. Some.

Danny How much?

Nicole I don't know. Some.

Danny (*pause*) Well how long did you feed him for?

Nicole Ten minutes? Fifteen?

Danny And he fed all that time?

Nicole Most of it.

Danny (*pause*) So you think he's OK?

Nicole His stomach is the size of a two-pence piece.
I read that. He doesn't need that much. And he's getting
something.

Danny But how much?

Nicole I don't know.

Danny (*pause*) And are you still bleeding?

Nicole It's fine. It's normal.

Danny I don't think it's normal.

Nicole Sorry, are you a doctor?

Danny I'm just saying.

Nicole He's here. It doesn't matter. Nothing matters.
He's here.

Danny You shouldn't be bleeding.

Nicole It's fine. Happens to loads of mums. I'm fair-
skinned. So they're sensitive. You know that. We just
have to get used to each other. It's new for both of us.
Once he settles into it, we'll be fine.

Danny But what if he doesn't?

Nicole He will. (*Pause.*) And it's what he needs. (*Pause.*)
I was reading. It's amazing. All the facts. D'you know
that when a baby is sick, the baby's saliva stimulates the
breast to make antibodies specific to that illness. That
illness. Isn't that incredible? And it's like, the milk I'm

getting now, you couldn't make it, you couldn't go into a lab and make it. It's extraordinary, it's got all these antioxidants and proteins and it just happens. It's exactly, exactly what he needs and it just happens. Day one.

Danny But if it's not working.

Nicole Who says it's not working?

Danny He's still hungry, Nic.

Nicole (*pause*) So you don't want to hear my poem then?

SCENE TWENTY-TWO

The prefab.
   Cyril sits, breathing hard.
   May's body is still in her chair, now covered with a single white sheet.

Cyril No use. Ground's like stone. Couldn't even get a foot down. And there's pipes. And I'd have to bury you deep. The dogs. Foxes. Sniff you out. (*Pause.*) When I'm gone they'll knock this place down, build those flats, all the young people coming in. And they'll never know we'd been here, lived here, been happy here. Never know where Douglas sat on his blanket, where we planted his tree. They'll dig all that up, his tree, and all his toys, all that we buried. (*Pause.*) So what am I gonna do with you, sweetheart? Don't want you buried in some unknown land, people coming in here, dragging you off, you'd hate that. Cold hands on you, tag on your foot. Pushed down some corridor by some porter dropping his breath on you. (*Pause.*) Can't keep you, I know that. Been days now. I'd like to, like to put you in my pocket, carry you with me in a matchbox, keep you close. (*Pause.*) 'Cause I'm frozen, May, don't know which way is up, I can feel my bones getting brittle, feel God descending on me, counting up my sins. (*Pause.*) And if I knew, I'd go. If I knew I'd get to see you both, I'd go. Take a pill, if I knew. (*Pause.*) So where am I gonna put you, May? What am I gonna do with you?

SCENE TWENTY-THREE

The school.
   Ash and Steph both hold sheets of A4.
   They're slightly wary of each other, awkward.

Steph B.

Ash B plus.

Steph 'Cause you said 'shit'. He loves all that.

Ash (*pause*) So you OK?

Steph Yeah. Totally.

Ash Haven't seen you.

Steph Seeing me now.

Ash (*pause*) I went round your house.

Steph I know. My mum told me.

Ash Said you weren't in.

Steph I know.

Ash (*pause*) Were you out?

Steph (*pause*) Seeing someone. This guy.

Ash Who?

Steph Can't tell you.

Ash Who?

Steph Just told you. Can't tell you. (*Pause.*) He's married.

Ash He's what?

Steph Gonna leave his wife though. She's just like dead old, and they don't even have sex or nothing. Wants me to chuck school so we can be together. Get a flat.

Ash He's married?

Steph And he's tall, used to be an athlete.

Ash So what's he doing with you?

Steph (*pause*) He can't help himself. It's physical.

Ash (*pause*) So where d'you meet him?

Steph Outside this club. He just comes up to me. Asks for a cigarette. Then he kisses me. (*Pause.*) And he's got a car.

Ash And you're seeing him?

Steph Just told you.

Ash So who is he?

Steph Can't tell you.

Ash (*pause*) Are you . . .

Steph What? He's a man. What do you think?

Ash That's not even legal.

Steph Fuck, you sound like my mum.

Ash Well, what is wrong with you?

Steph What's wrong with *you*? (*Pause.*) Are you sad?

Ash Sad?

Steph I'm seeing someone else.

Ash No. Fuck that. (*Pause.*) I'm starting tae kwon do Tuesday. So, whatever.

SCENE TWENTY-FOUR

The IKEA flat.

Nicole sits. The baby cries through the baby monitor; it's switched to silent but the red LEDs continue to flash.

Danny comes in. He places a full baby's bottle of milk next to Nicole.

After a moment he leaves.

Nicole just stares at the bottle.

She takes it, feels its warmth, gently shakes it.

Then she unscrews the top and drinks it down in one, retching as she does so.

Meanwhile the LEDs have become a silent, solid block of red as the baby screams.

SCENE TWENTY-FIVE

Cyril and May.

May's body is still in her chair. Only her feet are visible.

Cyril Just bones, in cloth. And quiet. Stench of burning. Don't know why I'm thinking of it now. Knees, elbows, big heads, shaved. Couldn't look. Had to look. One boy was twitching, think it was a boy, got that thin there were no boys, no girls. Not dead though, but past living. And not sad nor crying nor scared, not even thinking, just eyes up to heaven, emptied out, everything emptied out. He was right at my foot and I says to my pal, 'Shoot it, give it a bullet to let it go,' but he couldn't. (*Pause.*) And I couldn't. Could kill a big bloke, big German, all fat and lardy, put a bayonet through that, but this . . . Well, you can't kill a thing that can't live. So we walked on. And there were so many.

SCENE TWENTY-SIX

The IKEA flat.

Nicole sits. In front of her is a baby's bottle full of milk.

Behind her sits the baby monitor. Baby cries loudly through it, turning the LED lights bright red.

Danny comes in.

He flicks a switch on the baby monitor. The sound goes off but the line of LED lights continues to flicker red.

Danny He's crying.

Nicole I know he's crying, I don't need to hear him crying to know he's crying. (*The bottle.*) And take that away please.

Danny He's been crying solid for half an hour.

Nicole So pick him up.

Danny He doesn't want me, he wants you.

Nicole Comfort him.

Danny He doesn't want comfort. He wants food.

Nicole . . .

Danny (*pause*) How much has he had? (*Pause.*) He doesn't sound right, Nic, his breathing. He's getting dehydrated. I need to give him something.

Nicole No, you don't.

Danny He is going to get ill. Is that what you want? (*Pause.*) You need to talk to someone.

Nicole I don't need to talk to someone. I need to feed my baby.

Danny So feed him. Or let me feed him.

Nicole No! Don't you dare. I'm his mother. Me. Not you. I am full of milk, I'm leaking, I've got breasts like a fucking cow, he is not going on that bottle.

Danny He has to eat.

Nicole From me. Once you go on bottles that's it. He won't go back. He won't have me ever again.

Danny You're feeding him blood.

Nicole Not just blood. He's getting something.

Danny He's getting blood.

Nicole I need to give him something, empty something into him. I need to do that.

Danny You can. Just express. Use the pump, it would still be you, your milk.

Nicole I don't want to give my love to a pump, I want his mouth, on me.

Danny (*pause*) Let's get someone round.

Nicole I don't want someone round.

Danny You can't keep doing this.

Nicole I am going to be his mother.

Danny You are his mother, you just can't feed him. It happens.

Nicole Well, it's not going to happen to me. (*Pause.*) Something's wrong, with him, or . . . I see all those mothers, tits shoved in their fat babies, chatting, coffee with friends. If they can do it, why can't I? I am full of milk, his milk, so why doesn't he want it?

Danny He just can't latch on right. Like she said. It's his tongue, or his jaw, it's normal.

Nicole We should phone a doctor, a different doctor. Our doctor hardly even looked at him.

Danny 'Cause there's nothing wrong with him.

Nicole Well, maybe it's the wrong baby then, that happens.

Danny Jesus, Nic, can you hear yourself?

Nicole You weren't even there! And that ward was filthy, and those nurses. He's probably got something, some disease.

Danny There is nothing wrong with him.

Nicole So why can't I feed him?! Why doesn't he want me!

SCENE TWENTY-SEVEN

Cyril is pouring petrol from an old tin can over the bundle that May is under.

Cyril And you'll be warm, sweetheart, first time in a long time, right through to your bones. I don't want people touching you. You'd hate that. And this is what you wanted. Always said. (*Pause.*) I'll be fine. Just find a corner. Curl up. Wait.

Pause. He rests.

Always loved the smell of petrol, smells like something is going to happen. In the tank, loved all those smells. Back then. (*Pause.*) Saw men burn in there, got so hot, there was nothing left to bury. Just turned to smoke and drifted off. (*Pause.*) Best way to go, sweetheart, straight to the clouds.

He strikes a match.

SCENE TWENTY-EIGHT

The park.

Ash stands by the duck pond, eating a whole chicken. He's forcing it down now, not enjoying it. After a moment he becomes aware that he is being watched.

Cyril stands about twenty feet away, staring at Ash.

Cyril's hands, and the front of his coat are black, singed. He holds a bottle of bleach.

Ash What? (*Pause.*) You want some? You can't have it. (*Pause.*) And yeah, I am gonna eat this whole chicken, even though I am truly fucking sick of eating fucking chicken. (*Pause.*) My girlfriend likes big men. She is genetically programmed to think about fat babies, so I'm supposed to look like a fucking wrestler, and I am never gonna look like a fucking wrestler unless I eat a lotta fucking chicken. (*Pause.*) And why does everyone look at me when I'm eating chicken? (*Pause.*) Will you stop looking at me!

Cyril I got a knife.

Ash Why you gotta knife?

Cyril And I'm not scared.

Ash I don't want you to be scared. I just don't want you looking at me when I'm eating chicken. (*Pause.*) What's up with your hands?

Cyril . . .

Ash spots the bottle of bleach.

Ash And what's that? Why you got that?

Cyril Bleach. For the dogs. You live here?

Ash Bleach? Wait, don't you be bleaching any dogs. They'll lock you up, what is wrong with you?

Cyril You live here?

Ash What, in the park?

Cyril Round here.

Ash Yeah.

Cyril I can't find the police station. I need the police station. Want to turn myself in.

Ash Why? What you done?

Cyril My wife.

Ash What you done to your wife?

Cyril She's gone.

Ash Where's she gone?

Cyril She's dead! Are you soft in the head or something? I need a police station. Want it finished.

Ash Why's she dead?

Cyril 'Cause she died.

Ash What happened to her?

Cyril Look at my hands! You seen my hands? I need a police station.

Ash You need a doctor.

Cyril Police station!

Ash Alright. Police station. Straight back out the park. Left, and just keep walking. (*Pause.*) D'you want me to show you?

Cyril I'll find it.

Ash Just follow the road.

Cyril I'll find it.

Ash I could show you.

Cyril I'll find it! I've been to Berlin in a tank. You done that?

He goes. Ash calls after him.

Ash Just don't be bleaching any dogs.

Ash looks at his chicken, repulsed, then wraps it up. He's had enough.
His phone goes. He takes it out.

SCENE TWENTY-NINE

Steph's video goes viral.

SCENE THIRTY

The IKEA flat.
Nicole sits with her iPad. She watches the screen. We hear snippets of Steph's video as she flicks from place to place.
The baby monitor is silent, no flashing lights.

Steph (*on video*) . . . Were you hungry, Mr Doig? 'Cause that's how it felt –

Pause. Nicole flicks the iPad.

– when you kissed me, you turned me into a woman. So I want to give you something—

Nicole stops the video. Danny stands in the doorway.

Danny (*pause*) I've been suspended.

Nicole (*pause*) For *her*? For *that*? You've fucked up our life for *that*?

68

Danny It's not her fault.

Nicole She's titless. She looks like a boy. I mean, I knew you were frustrated, but Jesus . . .

Danny Ignore it.

Nicole And she's the reason.

Danny It's stupid. Ignore it.

Nicole Ignore it?

Danny Where's the baby?

Nicole How can I ignore it?

Danny Where is he, Nic?

Nicole Is that what you like?

Danny No, it's not what I like.

Nicole 'Cause I look at you and I don't really know. All these years. I just don't know, deep down, what the thing is you really crave.

Danny Not that.

Nicole And she's not even one of the pretty ones. I've seen some of those girls in the park, I would understand, but her . . .

Danny Did you feed him?

Nicole So was I just too old? Was that it?

Danny It was nothing.

Nicole *Mr Doig.* 'What you gave me, *Mr Doig.*' What you gave me. Your name. In her mouth. Like it's hers. And did you kiss her? She keeps saying it. So did you?

Danny Where is he?

Nicole It's a very simple fucking question. Did you kiss her?

Danny On the cheek.

Nicole So you did.

Danny On the cheek.

Nicole Why?

Danny Because she wanted me to. She asked me to.

Nicole So that's who you were thinking about? That's who you were thinking about when we made our baby?

Danny What?

Nicole Well, tell her to come and feed him, tell her to come and get chewed at till she bleeds. Tell her to come and be his fucking mother!

Danny He's got a mother.

Nicole Why did you do that!

Danny 'Cause I wanted something! Something. So I kissed her. But she was cold, and she was fourteen. There's no reason here, Nic, there's nothing to find. We made a baby, a beautiful baby, and you can't feed him like you want to. That's all there is. (*Pause.*) So what are you going to do? Are you going to let him die? Are you going to let him waste away till there's nothing left? (*Pause.*) There is no reason.

The baby monitor starts flashing red.

SCENE THIRTY-ONE

The street.
Steph stands waiting. She is not in uniform. She also wears a hat, hiding her hair.

Ash enters, still in uniform.

They acknowledge each other in silence, wary, awkward, then Steph takes a piece of paper out of her pocket. She reads.

Steph 'Meet outride KFC after scrool'. (*Pause.*) Question mark. (*Pause.*) Were you riding a bike or something?

Ash You need to get yourself a phone.

Steph Yeah, well, that's not gonna happen.

Ash (*pause*) You look different.

Steph Cut my hair. Bought a hat.

Ash Is it working?

Steph Dunno. Someone scratched 'slut' on my mum's car. She's not come out the house yet. Police said it's just, like, there now, online, for ever. (*Pause.*) And I look shit. (*Pause.*) This girl comes up to me, shoves her phone in my face and says, 'That's you,' and I says, 'That's not me, no way, she's got long hair, and she is *ugly*.' And she goes, 'Yeah, she is totally ugly.' (*Pause.*) Social worker says I'll have to move school. Haven't even done anything wrong.

Ash I never looked. Someone sent it to me, but I never looked.

Steph That's 'cause you're gay. (*Pause.*) Are you gay?

Ash Dunno. Don't think so. (*Pause.*) Why d'you send it to him?

Steph Thought he liked me. Just wanted, something.

Ash Did you . . .

Steph What do you think?

Ash (*pause*) So how'd Cas get it?

Steph Went through my phone. He's always doing that shit. Thinks it's funny.

Ash (*pause*) Heard you stabbed him.

Steph Compass. But I missed. This little first year comes up and goes, 'I've seen your tits, you've got no tits.' So I goes into Mr Summerfield's class and I get this compass and Cas is just laughing. (*Pause.*) Teaching assistant got me in a headlock. Had to sit in Miss Park's room and she keeps going, 'If you're pregnant, it's your own fault.'

Ash He's been suspended. Cas. (*Pause.*) I saw him. He works in Sports Direct. Went in yesterday, tried on like fifty pairs of trainers, then put them back in all the wrong boxes.

Steph You are so gay. (*Pause.*) Why d'you wanna see me? No one wants to see me.

Ash I gotta voucher.

Steph A voucher?

Ash Pizza Hut. Sicka fucking chicken. (*Pause.*) And I like you.

Steph (*pause*) I dunno.

Ash You gotta eat.

Steph People stare. Don't even hide it. Like I'm dirty. (*Pause.*) Sit next to me, they'll stare at you.

Ash So? Fuck 'em. I won't look. I'll just look at you, look at your face. (*Pause.*) You gotta nice face.

SCENE THIRTY-TWO

The IKEA flat.
  Nicole sits.
  The baby monitor is silent.
  The front door opens and closes.

Nicole (*calls out*) I don't want to do this. (*Pause.*) Please don't make me do this.

After a moment . . .
    Cyril walks tentatively in.
    Nicole stares.
    Danny follows.

(*To Cyril.*) Who are you?

Danny This is Cyril. Got a little bit lost. He was looking for the police station. I said I'd take him down there, but maybe he could just sit for a bit, get himself together.

Nicole Lost?

Cyril It's all changed, the streets, all different. Moved all the bus stops, knocked things down.

Nicole (*to Danny*) Can't you take him home?

Danny Not really. Just ten minutes. He hasn't had anything to eat for a while.

Cyril Tuesday.

Danny I'll get you something.

Cyril Got a baguette?

Danny I'll have a look. And I'll find the phone number, OK? For the police. (*To Cyril.*) Sit. Go on. We'll sort this out. (*To Nicole.*) He's fine. (*Pause.*) And I'm making up a bottle. And we're doing this. Now.

Nicole just looks away. Danny goes out to the kitchen.
    For a moment Nicole and Cyril are silent.

Nicole I'm Nicole. (*Pause.*) Are you OK? (*Pause.*) Your hands. What happened?

Cyril I set fire to my wife. (*Pause.*) And my house. (*Pause.*) She was dead. Didn't want people touching her.

Nicole (*pause*) Sorry, did this really happen?

Cyril Yes.

Nicole You set fire to your house?

Cyril Just a house.

Nicole And your wife?

Cyril Dead wife. In a chair.

Nicole (*pause*) Is there someone we could call?

Cyril Fire brigade?

Nicole I meant family. What about family?

Cyril Gone. Just me.

Nicole Children?

Cyril (*pause*) You live here?

Nicole Yes.

Cyril That your husband?

Nicole Yes.

Cyril And you've a baby?

Nicole Yes.

Cyril You're lucky. Best thing. Family.

Nicole (*pause*) This really happened?

Cyril Yes!

Nicole It's just, if you haven't eaten . . .

Cyril D'you think I'm mental? I was a soldier. I'm not mental.

Nicole (*pause*) So where are you going to go?

Cyril Prison. (*Obviously.*) Against the law to go burning things, even your own. Got nothing now anyway. All finished for me. That's my only possession. (*The bottle of bleach.*) For the dogs. Ninety-three, bottle of bleach. Can't be tucking that in at night.

Nicole They won't send you to prison.

Cyril They'll have to send me somewhere. I burned up my wife. That's not normal.

Nicole (*pause*) Maybe it was an accident. This fire.

Cyril I'm not mental. I just said.

Nicole (*pause*) What was her name? Your wife.

Cyril We had a baby. Little boy. Three years old he was. When we lost him.

Nicole I'm sorry.

Cyril You don't get past that. (*Pause.*) I'd be happy to go too. Drink this. (*The bleach.*) Can't even get the top off though.

Nicole What happened? Your little boy?

> *The baby starts to whimper through the monitor.*
> *For a moment Nicole and Cyril just listen.*
> *The whimper turns to a cry.*
> *Nobody moves.*

Cyril He wants feeding.

Nicole I know.

Cyril Know that cry. Remember that. My wee boy was always hungry. Hollow legs, that's what the wife said. (*Pause.*) Why don't you feed him? I'll go.

Nicole No.

Cyril So why don't you feed him?

Nicole . . .

Baby cries, getting louder, more insistent.

Cyril You should feed him. Why don't you feed him? Something wrong with you?

Nicole No. Nothing wrong. It just happens. I can't . . . I can't feed him, breastfeed him. It doesn't work. We don't work. Can't quite find a way past it, that's all.

Cyril My wife had that. They gave you a pill back then to stop the milk. She cried for a week, solid, more than the baby. But she loved him all the more for it. Don't be too hard on yourself, life's hard enough. You held him in your belly nine month, that's food. Kept him warm, that's food. Plenty ways to feed.

Nicole (*pause*) Your family. What were their names?

Danny comes in. He places a full baby's bottle on the table. He flicks off the monitor.

Danny (*to Cyril*) They said just come down. We'll get you something on the way.

Nicole (*to Danny*) Where are they going to put him?

Danny Not sure.

He goes back out. Cyril gets to his feet.

Cyril Hope they lock me up. Man should get what he deserves. (*Pause.*) May, that was my wife. Loved her very much. And Douglas, that was my wee boy. God took him, sent a bin lorry down Raglan Street. I had his hand, then he was gone.

Danny comes back in, carrying the baby.
For a moment Cyril simply stares, then turns to go.

Nicole Would you?

Cyril What?

Nicole Would you feed him, before you go?

Danny Nic?

Nicole Give him a bottle. Would you do that? I don't think I can.

Cyril Me?

Nicole Yes.

Cyril You don't know me.

Nicole I don't need to.

Cyril (*pause*) No. I'm an old man. I can't do that. Wouldn't know how to do that.

Nicole Just let him have it. He's hungry. He'll want it. (*To Danny.*) Please. Just the first time. (*To Cyril.*) Please.

Cyril My hands are black.

Nicole I don't care.

Cyril No. You don't know me, you don't know what I've done.

Nicole I do. You told me. Please. (*To Danny.*) Please. Just the first time.

Danny (*pause*) Is that what you need?

Nicole Yes.

Cyril I've never fed a baby.

Nicole Please.

Cyril doesn't move.

Danny Here.

He takes the bottle of bleach from Cyril.

I'll just bin this, yeah?

He leaves the bleach on the floor.

Sit. Go on. It's fine. It's good. (*To Nicole.*) It's all good.

Cyril sits. Danny carefully lifts the baby on to Cyril's lap.

Cyril What do I do?

Nicole I don't know. I've never done it.

Cyril I don't want to hurt him.

Danny You won't hurt him.

Nicole Just feed him. Let him take it.

Danny shakes the baby's bottle and hands it to Cyril.

Danny He's hungry enough. Trust me.

Cyril He's a tiny wee thing.

Danny You just need to hold his head.

Cyril What's his name?

Danny Dunno yet. Baby for now.

Cyril Baby.

Nicole Baby. (*Pause.*) And the milk should be warm.

Cyril Look at that.

Nicole Just warm.

Cyril That face. Looking right at me. Do I just . . .

Nicole I suppose so . . .

Danny (*pause*) Yeah . . .

Nicole Yeah . . . (*Pause.*) I guess you just . . .

Cyril gives the baby the bottle.
After a moment the crying gets quieter.
   Turns to a whimper.

Cyril Look at that.

The whimper starts to quieten . . .

He's taking it.

Then silence.

He's loving it. (*Pause.*) Look at that, May. That smile.
He's loving it.

Nicole He's hungry.

Cyril feeds the baby.
   A long silence.
   Baby feeds.
   Danny and Nicole watch.
   Cyril looks up.

Cyril He's beautiful.

The lights slowly fade.

End.